C000131988

Eighteen Poems

EIGHTEEN POEMS

SIMON JARVIS

 EYEWEAR PUBLISHING

First published in 2012
by Eyewear Publishing Ltd
74 Leith Mansions, Grantully Road
London W9 1LJ
United Kingdom

Typeset with graphic design by Edwin Smet
Author photograph by Finn Jarvis
Printed in England by TJ International Ltd, Padstow, Cornwall

ISBN 978-1-908998-03-3

WWW.EYEWEARPUBLISHING.COM

Simon Jarvis was born in 1963.
He is the Gorley Putt Professor of Poetry and Poetics at the
University of Cambridge. His previous books of verse are *The
Unconditional: A Lyric* (Barque, 2005), F_0 (Equipage, 2007) and
*Dionysus Crucified: Choral Lyric for Two Soloists and
Messenger* (Grasp, 2011).

Table of Contents

Lessons and Carols

The ring road rests, and frost settles over the meadow;
  down at the river the lights are strung out into faint
points of attention, and silence envelops the dark.
  Here I am standing again on the path at the edge of the city.
Here I am, set with a face looking up at the black
  exit from lighting, the place where the money runs out.
Over its pitch play the brilliant white invitations
  offered to everyone, sent to all sources of cash.
Kindness and tenderness bury themselves in these flaring
  or constantly blazing and unconscious characters
written in unfading colours upon the resilient jet.
  Earth's ancient rocks burning up into placards and beacons
cease into scarlets and oranges, bearing their message all night.

Where shall I walk now, if not into darkness and silence?
  Where shall I walk so as not to be drawn by the lit
emblems and tokens, the winning array? All the new gifts
  stand in the windows awaiting a look or a purchase,
stand in the flood of illumining phosphors and glass.
  While they are there they are not there: they are in suspended
transvalued inertia, lacking a use, and their properties
  turn from the light, while habitual prosopopeias
face them with magical attributes, turning them blind
  just where they stare at us, holding their eyeless fixation
into our faces, these eyed ones, these equally blank
  caverns or sockets, these natural organs, surrendered
up to this table, these miniature plinths in the window

folded in silks or in velvets and holding their grimace
  towards the indifferent or longing beholder who fears not to
pacify each of their hatreds, fears their concerted displeasures.
  Each knows us, sees us. Although we can never believe it,
under this laboured neutrality works a persisting
  terror of scorning them, terror of giving offence to them.
We must buy gifts; we must come to the store,
  leaving our monoglot offerings there at the checkout,
leaving with objects apparently filled up with life.

How they can sing, can wheedle and tick and can rhyme
winningly to us, as though all we lose for them were
     well lost, and given us only to lose in this way.
How sweet that hour is, the hour of the glimmering twilight,

hour of the sodium suddenly colouring water
     left in the pavement, and flitting from there to the windows,
placing its oranges almost unseen on display
     cases and fittings. How sweetly it deepens the sky
into its darker pale blue, to its royal then cobalt
     seen at the edge of the blackening gables, whose shadows
stand with inherited umbers, where Tudor or Caroline
     houses hold in their new stomachs, their dazzle of shop:
each an enchanted remainder which gazes away
     to the vanishing light-source, *Kulturlandschaft* marked by the sun
as a castle or foreground past which I may look to the west
     carrying with me these goods which I bear from the field
back to the hearth, to the cooker, the warm kitchen table.

That they are truly demonic is too hard to know.
     Since there is nothing demonic, they cannot be.
Just as I know that my pacifications are mine,
     just as I know that the cooker, the warm kitchen table
are things among others, so I must know that the jewels,
     the glamoured toy car with its surface of shimmering purple,
the telephone smooth as a baby, the shallow recessed
     hand-holds which welcome me into my family car,
all are quite empty of thought or of motive: all, all
     think nothing at all, more than a stone thinks, or less than it.
All that I feel for them floats in an ether of foolish
     half-waking conjecture, cutting the circuit short just
where thought might become painful, might tell me how to wake up.

Who are the gifts for? Mine for my own, for my loved ones,
     yours for your loved ones too, for your own dear loves and kin.
Deeply we tie ourselves using them deep into love,
     deeply they bury their spirits inside us and sing to return.
Just at the sight of their wrappings and trimmings I love
     as though I were tied to those ancestors I have forgotten.

Each wishes to be an exception. Each glittering package
  wishes to be a cathedral imprisoning heaven.
They must stand there; they must remain and wait
  steadfastly into the morning, or otherwise something will die,
something will come round to finish us off in the night.
  So as the packages stand straining blessedly out
every comfort they offer suppresses a fear.

Just as a father who wishes to comfort his children
  tells them that spirits are fictions and cannot appear;
just as a father who wants to protect his dear children
  holds them against him, enfolds them in cuddles, for fear
that his own strength will be too small to save them all, knowing
  he floats like a twig in a river of pitiless money,
knowing he is himself pitiless, money itself without malice,
  just as the child hears the song of the fairy prince singing
there past his father's embrace, there in the dark street outside,
  knowing at once in these spiritual tunes the sound of what comes
straight from the other world, straight from enchantment and straight
  from the terrible kingdom of non-love, of freedom and absence and longing,
so do these presents stand vigilant there by the window.

The spirits are fictions; the gifts are their counter-fictions.
  Now as before, as I stand at the edge of the city,
I stare at the offers of kindness, the prospects of colour and warmth.
  Why should I not like these colours, these lit invitations?
I have accepted them all; I have eaten the meal of indifference
  day in and day out; I have wished for love's soviet state
only in theory, while with my teeth and prostheses
  I have in practice still wished for non-love, for the kingdom of unliving spirits.
It is too dark to walk down the lane at the edge of the city.
  I must get back to my wife and my children, my loved ones.
May the bereft state continue its care for our welfare
  there in the dark, where its artless security shines!
I shall go walking back home, while these measures and lines
  borrow some part of their tune from the fictional spirits.

Night Office

Every last person in this book is dead,—
including me. I'm talking to you, yes,
thanks to my poet; he, thanks to me; my head
shakes and reverberates, while, less and less,
the waves of sound diminish, and, instead,
a lasting silence fills me, and I rest.
Now in this blackness I begin to sing.
Invisible is every little thing:

all, all, invisible, but that, just there,
right at the far end of the long thin room,
there where the curtain is ajar, I stare
into the night, all night, as one for whom
all locomotion is impossible, and where
that thin gap stands, I watch when through the gloom
flake after flake of trembling distant snow
falls to the ground where I can never go.

They fall so calmly and so thickly; each
wavers yet drops directly to the ground.
They drift and cluster, like the purest speech
freed from all causes of dislike, whose sound
gathers, disperses, lets its easy reach
range freely through whatever thoughts are found
left in the air, available as breathing,
or in the open page whose quick conceiving

lets all surmises leave their prints and tracks
deep in its whiteness, where their pressures write.
Then, just as surely, these determined blacks
are filled by flake and flake, until the light
unthinking action of the snow conceals
every last record, and the gazer lacks
all means to know their having been. The night
welcomes and hides them: what each thinks or feels

is as obliterated as a name
drawn in the soft sand when repeated waves
delete at one stroke its uncertain fame,
leaving these empty flats. The corner where one shaves
is still invisible. The mirror in its frame
glimmers more darkly, where its pool just saves
the snow's dim lights into its silver, and
they fall more slowly over by the stand.

Dead, every one, and gone beneath the snow.
I search the past for them, but miss their faces.
They are where all the happy dead must go.
Only, in this dark room, I cannot know
their quietness, their sleep; my head replaces
each one precisely in his life, and so
they walk again this path from lungs to teeth,
escaping painfully from sweet relief.

Each bears his rhythm like an inner star:
each is walked through by some one line of stress
not chosen or invented, though they are
not accidental either, since they test,
for each imprinted pattern, where the bar
is lightly crossed, or halted at. My chest
rises and falls beneath my shirt, as each
treads slowly through me his peculiar speech,

sending me softly dumbnesses, impressions
left in the surface of my slow tongue, which
shifts shape a little each time. Dreams, depressions,
pass through my face from inside. In this rich,
yet monochrome, design, these curls, recessions,
vaults and returns speak, soundlessly, dip, pitch
their friendly spirit voices through my sight
and out into the European night.

Fixed to the chair, I feel their pressure pass,
each with his proper contour, and they grow,
diminishing the ornamental brass,
the wallpapers and carpets, since I know,
at every stress, each failed protracted task
pushed by each voice along its own and slow
life-prolonged expirations, and its worked
reasons of sound, its still unshirked

necessities of fear, desire and pain.
Tonight one little tune won't leave my head.
It rattles through again and then again,
sitting me upright by this sleepless bed.
I do not want the snow to turn to rain.
I search the adits of my empty head
to know its source; I turn my recollections
over and over in their wrong selections,

till I detect this pattering refrain.
Ten years ago I walked across the bridge
over the river in the freezing rain.
It would not turn to snow; the distant ridge
refused to whiten, while the ice again
greeted my neck, my foot just slipped, then slid
along the pavement, swerved, and then recovered,
right at that moment when there was discovered

just in the corner of my eye the vast cathedral,
too large for its believers, and just now
dwarfing small clumps of them in polyhedral
splendours and gestures. Its bright sharpened bow
went sailing through the night, to put down evil
wherever it might surface, so that how
this back of it disgorged the faithful, few
at this cold, minor, festival, and who

they were, could not be seen, but, from its gaps
immensities of music opened, and their wide
curves, flights and logics, rivets, knots and straps
let the machine preposterously ride
out into air, let open all its taps,
until the flood of harmony inside
burst on the courtyard, and its unheard shape
drew in my listening. I heard escape

the improvisor's long preliminary
repreparation for the full return
first of his theme, which he would twist or vary
in strong chromaticisms, whose each turn
hammered new wishfulness, so the unwary
or somnolescent churchgoer must learn
new cadences accompanying each loved tune
just in time finally to rhyme with June

December's treasures of the shortest day,
the snow-filled and the snow-transfigured city
recalling to us what we could not say
had ever happened to us . . . Hope and pity
were swiftly summoned in the very way
the dominant collapsed, as though some witty
turn had revealed an unsuspected luck,
just waiting for us there. A passing truck

shook the whole road outside; at just that bar
the whole array roared up its triumph; then
its chords bashed out the tune, as to who are
in urgent need of help, or who are men
sleepwalking to a cliff—*Wach auf*, its far
and faint appeal calls through these ten years when
I think of it, as I do now, while snow
falls down and down to where I cannot go.

That tune's return was like a doctor's fist
beating and beating on the patient's heart.
Its blows rained down upon us, where they missed
their stony targets. Breaking on each part—
Adeste—dead men—*faithful souls*—then—this
refrain, with elephantine grandeur, starts,
flogging the dead horse of the past to life,
opening all breasts with its jagged knife.

That tune is not the one that I can hear.
A different line is running in my head.
It has no music; it is spoken, clear;
at any minute I will recollect
exactly what it is, and then its dear,
yet bitter, knowledge, will correct
this written memory, however sweet.—
V poslednij raz vam muzyka slushit.—

'For the last time you can hear music'. Yes,
that was the sound of it, but were those words
just the correct ones, was what they profess
just the real thought I had, when those loud thirds
and sevenths brought me almost to confess,
to say 'descended into hell' (absurd)
and bring me to the bread and wine to eat?—
V poslednij raz vam vera pozvonit,—

'for the last time faith sounds out to you'. Spoken
or as though whispered to me in the night
that line came to me like the unawoken
presentiment of total loss, foresight
whose truth I taste just here, in broken
breath, not now bread. It was the right
premonitory cadence, even though
I now mismingle it with Cochereau,

who wants to bring back life with heel and fist,
unelegiac or resuscitating
desperate harmonies—where what we miss
would be returned in total, thus belating
each moment of our having it, since this
adds to redemption one prosthesis hating
the lack of it, and that descanting anger
spoils in the music all its better, stranger,

lightness of luck, its free or easy yoke.
These lines of verse, however, know just that.
They have no descant, lack that holy smoke.
They travel on without a sharp or flat.
There is no point, no terminating joke.
They move along until the moment at
which they stop moving, and the poem ends.
They make infinitesimal amends

for long stupidity and cruelty;
they heal with true intelligence a wound
whose false need closes, so that we can see
all its wrong urgency, its late and soon
merely released, abandoned and set free
into what I should hardly call a tune.
I sit here in the dark, and through my bones
each instant of me rocks with silent tones.

There is no last time, but there is for me.
Each time this starts, I want to make it stop.
A stupid habit settles into me,
letting me wish to falter, fail and drop.
I want to pacify the quick unfree
leaps of my throat, to muffle at the top
each pain-fed melody, each real perception,
dispel each nerve into some long deception.

The Last Encounter—but no poem bears
that heading: all their hues and shades
leap at the first, whose recollection spares
colours, deleted from this poem, trades
its brilliants and its perfumes and its shares
quickly and glisteringly, or lights glades
richly from inside, so we wish to enter
and lose ourselves into its very centre.

So the electric candles, iridescing,
cast their imagined glances on a neck
whose lovely owner bends and dips, expressing
an unattainable perfection, decked
with some few ornaments, as though confessing
light's whole strong spectrum, where we can't inspect
an unmixed colour, but where all must mingle
round her whose beauty may alone stay single

in opera glasses or unconscious stares
from the police chief or the maestro, since
all eyes must fall on her whose light impairs
all other sources here, immortal glints
seducing into truth with silken snares
who will become the necessary prince
detained, imprisoned, tortured and beheaded
to serve that justice to which he was wedded,

while fair Sophia leaves the city, and
is never seen again, except in stories
told in some damp apartments. Stand
and turn the gas down. Little glories
of flame play round the vent. *Russkij Kharbin!*
you are deleted, like the Severn Tories
or like the works of Golokhvastov, and
your coteries, claques, guilds of poets, spleen

and ideals, and Pereleshin hearing
halfway to Rio the Parisian note,
its godforsaken whisper, in some clearing
like Hongbo Square where you could still see float
the pyramided roofs whose bulbs thrust, spearing
into the flat white of the cold sky. Throat,
revive that bench! Speak failing pages of *Rubezh*,
verse brought from Moscow or from Voronezh

along the Chinese Eastern Railway, holding
rhyme to its most exact requirement, set
just at each terminal, and there enfolding
whatever of indelible is met
between its clasps: so when the scolding
Young Guards come and destroy the church, you get
your bags, and, then, the Berlitz School and British
Council, one librarian; so skittish

monks know their Solovyov, Bely, Kuzmin:
each is chewed up into the heart, as glances
may leave more understanding than words mean
in some precisely calculated trances
you fall to *On The Path*, which, first (Kharbin,
in 1937) let some dances
of tooth and lip slip into permanent
black rescue from the all impermanent

condition of continuous deletion
as which life cannot not strike us today.
Cannot not strike me, since my deep accretion
of cherished wounds and grievances must play
into each moment, to each new secretion
of its decomposition, or I say
psalms of a measureless outside, a tic
I can't get rid of, a compulsion, click.

I by privations register its strict
command of disenchantment: I strip down
each needless colour, and I then inflict
on every thought this tune, I build this town
of chastened melody in air, delict
of stripes on print, until I with a frown
burn each vast poem and commit its ghost
to the most perishable folded host

of lobes and nodes and trackless little gaps
in my head's one left organ. Then, this done,
I start again. I reconvene my maps,
placing thought's flag in every city: one
in Riga, one in Prag, another flaps
at Nice, at Cairo, as the whole undone
series of dead men marches: Biarritz,
where Blok fed cigarette ends to the crabs

or thought about Sophia, sometimes, drifting
in miserable consciousness of ending
drunk or indifferent on the sands whose shifting
could not be patterned, since their hot unending
slides of mere silica evade all sifting
and four feet fail before the neverending
task of its comprehension, take the fag,
or die entangled in a plastic bag,

you're history, which means, you are not, shed
into the cold and meaningless Atlantic.
A proper name I speak inside my head
relieves me for one instant from this frantic
fury of disappearance, as, instead
of the police, I reconvoke some antic
precisions of a possible unknowing
at just what speed the whole damned thing is going

down to the pit and to prosperity.
Hell's cicerone, I yet may not remember
just where each special circle is; for me,
each more particular revenging ember
loses its name, and I can hardly see
whether in this perpetual November
this or that word burn fastest: where they stop
may be perdition's nadir or its top.

The disestablished State! This Brobdingnag!
The National Mall: the national mausoleum!
You cannot walk in it without you gag
on nothing's ashes, since each big museum
rears up on pyramids: each über-flag
reminds you of the tortured perineum
of each outlaw this law's dead heart spat out
into that lawlessness it cannot live without.

Earth knows a port of Hell: the world's free hatreds
collect into continuous surveillance.
Privation's vast sarcophagus, one fated
parade of lack-love lenses, whose dumb valence
presses this diorama of unsated
pursuit of happiness into the palest
abashed sky fading like the thinnest screen
down to the ocean, to the lost machine.

Why should this shake me, but that each shocked stretch
of shrinking skin at once reviles and owns it?
Why must I shudder, why turn cold and retch
but cold law made the warm heart which disowns it?
All frenzied self-conceit would gladly fetch
itself to some sweet kingdom: what erodes it
is hard self-knowledge, when the soul's broke Lego
spells in pink shards its *In Arcadia Ego*.

I must inevitably imitate
those good machines which are the friendly powers
sustaining each new luxury, each spate
of abstract freedoms which I burn like hours:
I 'have to switch off', must convert to fate
intolerable life, just 'shut down'; towers
at the horizon do not fall but glisten,
shining with each fact to which they can't listen:

since the elusive central fear I felt
when I beheld in Washington the tops,
the faux-Phocion backdrop, felt life melt
down to that zero, as a hanged man drops
to satisfy his public, or a welt
spreads on the smacked face, so these doors, gift shops,
were the truth coming from the ancient state
to wake me from my life, and come too late.

In theory I should like to drive a car
through every inch of it, & each motel
should let its lettering eclipse each star
invisible above, & each hotel,
each pool, each parking lot, each lobby, bar
should with reiterated speech go tell
numbers by numbers of appealing freedoms
refusing to divulge their needed reasons.

This is the kind of thing I think I want.
Impersonality in person, sent
in free parabolas, a blank descant
on no tune under them, so that each front
ascends from measure, and the pale or faint
glitter of phosphor is a lonely tint
delighting lovelessly in all that can't
confine or even know it, so it won't

ask for the check or point out that the cloud
is made of water as it floats and spools across
my black sedan in little. Disallowed:
this makes the charm of each recorded loss
whose passing I may not lament, aloud.
I watch each helpless image run across
the hood, then disappear into the night.
Goodbye from now to being in the right,

farewell to lofty projects. Literature
became repulsive to me long before
I died; and so the topics of my pure
deliria recalled both less and more
than some minute particular: each sure
moment or colour lost its clear allure
because "there are no longer any sounds.
Can it be you don't hear this?" What resounds

is information, and its instant travels
on the erased earth's surface, where I rest.
The first known minute when a life unravels:
pain's matchless instance, pain's unholy test.
The long car leaving on the graded gravels;
a failing in your face; flight, or arrest;
the morning when you cannot go to work,
pinned to the bed. The broken cheek must shirk,

today, each smallest meeting, flinch or shrink.
Verse is the catalogue of thought corrosions.
It is not that I wish or even think
to bring an end to these required explosions;
I only wish to so deploy this ink
that each be partnered with the right implosions
compacting passion at that soldered letter
fixed to the spirit which it best can fetter.

I am the instigator: I set fire,
not douse it, when I clip each needless word;
in me those sounds which cannot be for hire
settle in each head where they first were heard.
I from the middle of a quenchless pyre
burn irreversibly, as though referred
from flame to flame in order to preserve
combusting life whose perishable swerve

fails always, never to be once extinguished,
and, when it fails, ignites its unrelinquished
light in that dark which may not be distinguished.

Colloquium

Ten miles below the polar ice
exists a rock that praises Christ.

Beneath imperishable white
it sings a hymn throughout the night.

All life and colour there contract
into impassioned parts of black.

It grumbles for its daily bread.
It is unquestionably dead.

I wrap it up in furs and felt.
Ten miles above, the ice caps melt.

After Afanasy Fet

All that I feel, I feel more acutely at night, and every
    image, fearful and mute, trembles sustained in the dark:
Sound itself is more palpable also when, then, without moving
    I hold in my hands some small book, running in thought through all
that's impossible-possible, strange-and-habitual. The lamp
    burns low at my bedside, the moon visits me through the window,
then suddenly, distantly, sings out a bell—and quietly
    into my bedroom the sounds come floating. I wholly surrender.
The heart discovers in them, in these sounds, a peculiar dampness,
    precisely as though they had been washed in dew in the night.
The sound sings on still, although each time returning as altered:
    now it is heavy with bronze, now richer in silver.
Strange how my ear at this moment can hear without listening;
    thinking of something quite different, still in my mind there is wave after wave
while a still deeper and more secret power embraces
    the lamp, and the sounds, and the night; they dissolve into one.
So into colourfast blossoms of damp and somniferous poppy
    sometimes the midnight will drop an invisible dream.

After Batiushkov

A breath of summer air is blown
   over my silent cheek.
I wake, but not to happiness.
   I hardly see the weak
return of light into the sky,
   nor hear the horn which sounds
across the meadows or the bay.
   My loss alone shall speak.
Nothing can mend the failing heart,
   nor may cold words repair
with intellection or with art
   habitual despair.

After Kuzmin

Tea's steam disperses, and I see Mt. Fuji:
a gold volcano on a yellow sky.
The dish compresses nature to a circle;
tea-ripples quiver; and the sun's ant's eye
looks through these feathers of extended cloud
where black tea leaves are either birds or fish
delineating topaz in the azure
to have spring fit into a little dish.
The almond breathes its perfume; one far horn
echoes across the china: but, just here,
this unanticipated branch of a mimosa
falls from the rim and interrupts the sky
just as if on a page of Hegel's *Logic*
a line of Swinburne happened to pass by.

After Pushkin

A bell sounds, and I drop the book.
The line dries out upon my lips.
It floats before it fails and dips
below the reach of listening.
The sound comes from the parking strip.
My enemy, my tune, my fear,
who sees into me with a single look,
how did you know to find me here?

After Khodasevich

Like the full moon my soul shines bright.
It is as cold and clear and white.

There in the sky it burns and burns.
It never wants for me, or turns

a single glance in my direction.
It may not make the least reflection

on what I feel or undergo.
These things it was not born to know.

There are some words I can't forget,
and so I keep repeating them.
They stare back at me from a set
continuously deleting them.

Now I love only what resolves
in irrecoverable air;
as clouds, like letters soon dissolved,
seem opposites to disrepair.

USA

I cannot get out of the car.
Still the sky blackens; in the west
thin strips of light repeat a test.
So, when you wish upon a star,
this much is true, if not the rest.
It makes no difference who you are.

The See of Ebbsfleet

Walk it from here. There is no pedestrian footway, so cross to the right;
   into these oncoming vehicles, looking each motorist right in the face,
hope in this way to be seen and be spared being mown down at once by the car.
   Known acres of mud must extend just a mile from here, but there is no way
to get there, unless you should know something first or be willing to follow a map.
   How many like me would prefer to walk hour upon hour into traffic
than to prepare for this trip and so ruin its possible happiness?
   It is a failure of nerve: it is set resolution for loss:
since I prefer to be given whatever just happens now than to arrange
   for my end or my goal, as this shoal of high cloud in the firmament
glitters and twists, as though messages were being sent to me,
   or the whole sky were resplendent with just its own light
and not with reflections of light from a foundering star.

That we come too late is our favourite story, that story which lets
   this first person plural be gathered and shadow us now from the light of the sun.
Here at this edge of the carriageway I can just see the magnificent
   cooling towers rear up in front of me, each with its high hyperbolic
totter of curve and its vastest incursion outfacing that sky which it blanks.
   They are the severing monument, they are the fortress of lateness,
which while we see we gape openly, thinking a perfect disjunction,
   thinking ourselves redismembered, remembering nothing at all.
All the grey water is shining with whiteness of sun,
   all the blue water reserved for a welcoming name:
walking towards it I bear in my body the amplitudes coming towards me,
   feel with my inner limbs every collision foregone or prevented.
These spirit-impacts preserve me: these guardian messengers stand

as in a force-field around me, and let me proceed on the flat land
   down to the centre, the bright cash-dispenser, the warm destination of lights.
I do really mean it is hard not to think that the sky must hold messages.
   It really is work to continue to write it off hour after hour,
the counter-cantata of willed disenchantment, determined deletion of what
   is there and appears, a worked inattention to colour and line
working deflections or swift interceptions of meaning
   so that I just may keep walking and not lose my tread
but march like an army towards irresistible purchase

as though its tag or subtotal were branded in front of my eyes
stamping the air like a trademark or a thought which is always
   held at the front and the top of the brain to command and to sacrifice
all grey digressions of will & all blue diversions of feeling.

There are no such colours of mental events or perceptions.
   Just for that reason I hold to my word of as if.
There are no such marks on my retina: perfect deceptions
   still need a literal ground from whose letter they leap with a swift
fire of surmise, of reflection, selection and irony.
   I am still walking along this loud road to the point.
Just as I turn or I go to turn here at a corner
   I look up right and can see at the top of the distance the sea.
My head is shaken: I must stand and look
   out where it crashes (but I cannot hear it) again and again on the sand
just as these waves of the moon-driven traffic come sounding again on my shore
   of continued attention: the ear I leave out for them
keeps me alive while I stand there and stare across fields to the sea.

I shall be late. I cannot get my legs to begin
   moving me off from this spot; I cannot seem to make
whatever pulse is required to impel me to travel
   arrive in my limbs. Now in the air I conjecture invisible lines
unravelling west from the sea and bisecting the oolite belts,
   running out over the clays and the sandstones and south to the chalk
downs and the airbases, silos and grain stores and the tunnels of cable and gas
   binding each word and each gesture into unfelt solidarity,
to delicate total dependencies still disavowed and disowned.
   The lines I configure have nothing to do with these networks.
They must shine with retained and reserved coloration
   even as each cuts indifferently over the worked
inhabited surface, the solid impervious map.

Each is the line of an ancient and modern refusal.
   Each demarcates the protection of what it must take to be that
sole universal attached to this single peculiar spot.
   It can do no other than stand here invisibly
as though it would consecrate grid sectors and their co-ordinates
   or as though +Andrew might in his saloon car come flying
to visit his oversight on any instance of error.

This is the nation erected uniquely on ruins.
As for each minster a sponsoring ruin was needed
    so must each minster be ruined in turn and the bureaux
stand in their places. The gift shops and turnstiles and galleries must
    overlook in electric command the dark aisles and the obsolete
niches they sponsor and which from my curious gaze

turn their averted inscriptions, awaiting a judgement to come.
    The see of Ebbsfleet: the invisible
hierarch-heaven-sent crimson, the bare thought of powerless majesty,
    the theory of cloud's inner substance, of what from the purples and indigos
massed in the sky to the west of me breaks and rejoices
    just as a word at the never-meant moment may break and recover
what in me drops and still languishes, falling to default again.
    Its reasons are hidden inside an inaudible whisper.
Its fears are recorded inside an impalpable crypt.
    All Ebbsfleet resounds with their absences, soundingly measures
its cells of stiff loyalty locked to those pieces of land
    since their assembly must be apostolical, holding
the red thread back to the quickening terrors of Egypt.

What as I stand at this place I may feel is invisible.
    No one can see it or make it be part of the world.
What I must think or surmise is the sheer indivisible
    wordless interior whose stupefaction is curled
up like the substrate of everything else which appears.
    I am turned around to the sky now, to the place where the sun
is not setting but earth turns to darkness away
    hiding her face like that sex which is barred and rejected
so that the retina catches these pinks and these other lights
    just like that organ whose every cell is selected
to make them look just like that, see that by luck or by rights
    imperial blazing of far and celestial light is invested
for twenty minutes until it give way to the night.

Persephone

Down to the sugar vertex, down to the end of the line,
    down to the worst nub knowing reversions as queer as desire,
down to the hub, the jammed centre whose deafened reversions repeat
    their tight disconnections implacably soldered to failsafe refusals of spirit:
down, down, I go down, I must dive or must plunge as I sit here exerting
    immovably rigid my fingers to fixed irretractable semaphores
each of which stands indestructibly lit in its box of neglect.
    This final circle is ice, though it glitter like fire.
All the sound icons whose each auscultatory treat
    is like an invisible picture of glitter, as if to dispirit
with pretty excitements my thought & to stop my thought hurting
    just as this paragraph so far imprisoned in metaphors
assuages conditions I took it to show and inspect
                            wrecks
down to a slump or a slough of delicious despond each design
    which might shelter the least intimation of help or escape.
Begin again, therefore!   Here I am meeting my friends,
    the cold and so sweet ones, the ones I may drop or pick up,
just as they matchingly pick me or drop from their ladder of mates
    me with sincerest abandon of rapturous wish or contempt.
Here we all are in the square of propitious diversion.
    Each little moniker plays on a theft or a rape.
Each with solicitous wittiness wishes to put off what ends
    the march of perpetual fun in an unwelcome cup
drunk by compulsion, extended by unappeased fates.
    I am not I when me just at the very attempt
to get up from this chair this chair through infernal inversion
                           checks
or sucks back to itself just that strength which I wish to assign
    to some elsewhere I merely conjecture. Persephone!
Are you there now, my not-love, my companion, discomfiture and dissolution?
    Are you there anywhere when you are there, or are you
not ever there when your presents are wrapped in their letters
    so tightly, they may not be opened, but strain towards God?
Are you the skin of you, stuck to the venom you stick with,
    burning in pain with the fire of unceasing telephony
which you might never remove from you since it are you in solution

liquidly pinioned in depthless extensions of blue?
So one might say that my rhythms and rhymes are not fetters
   but inescapable consciousness through the hot rod
of self-selved prosthesis, the I-stick I think with which
                    texts
text's blankest melodies into a number I sign.
   Now as you kindly inform me that you are the queen of the underworld
I for empirical heartburn must reach for my tea;
   gulps of hot tannin defer your unwelcome reminder of hell
sufficiently well to permit me to keep going down
   or forwards to whichever moment of knowledge I think must reveal
me cured or destroyed. I crash on for some hurt or some shock
   which I consider must irreversibly kill or redeem my still undeterred
bondage to bondlessness, which I imagine must be
   my first true ascent since the first apple-snack when I fell
down by one inch to the inch-chute inducting me down
   or which I think must renew us, conceal us and heal
into new breath and new song these intransitive verbs or these locked
                    necks
blocked every second in clicks whose repealed and refined
   image of sound is discarded towards my irrelevant ear.
Tell me, my sweet, my non-love, have you eaten the food of the dead?
   Crocuses, hyacinths, irises, lilies and roses
throng the low meadow whose glimmering grasses are dusk
   fields of persisting regret from which mortals may never return.
Have you consumed those unnameable berries or have you then sold
   your skin for narcotic erasure of pain and of fear
or imperfect oblivion down in your watery bed?
   Is there one stain on your face whose black bruising discloses
irretrievable loss of the human so that your dark husk
   must stand apart in indifferent calmness when mortals shall burn,
since they must burn, and all in the end that is left of them here are these gold
                    flecks
set in the mute jaw, this wealth they can never resign?
   My questions are breath which disperses in answerless air.
My thoughts are invisible life, which I will to embody
   in any wrong sign or perennial lump which perpetuates
still through the lit web of numbers my impulse which fades
   here from my soul but is held in a temple of code,
in a temple of strong desecrations we build and rebuild every day.

Now as spirit distributes itself into sticks and devices whose prayer
chatters incessantly through its electrical body
   so I must think this sand capital which as it eats and attenuates
all living labour and which with negations abrades
   all resources of gentle invention is still the abandoned abode
which unliving non-spirits inhabit as grey for the grey.
Sex
abstractly separates each of our avatars when we would close and confine
   in this matched consolation of sweet opposition our opposite life to the socket.
When Persephone catches a sound of my lecture she listens straight past it to hear
   the hard numbers beneath it which for us or for her are the essence concealed,
a cadaver of sponsoring ribcage below the impertinent skin.
   When I say life she reads death for it since there is no diamond border
to render this difference safe from her dexterous knitting which ravels
   each infinite organ back to its sheath, to its natural pocket.
All this she does with the flick of an eyelid whose sheer
   disenchantment enlightens me just when it finds me revealed
wrong in the tip of my pixel or clicked up a thin
   strip of mined data: I must store up against this disorder
or set against all this dire fabric which twists and retorts and unravels a
hex
of besieged and recalcitrant consciousness, or lose my mind.
   "Yes, your sad Alamo skulks in that glorious ditch
"which if you merely relinquished, light airs and cool brooks should refresh you!
   "Yes, your invented Persephone is the barbarian host
"strong at the doors of perception, ready to burn down a skull
   "you insist must contain and protect that frail brain
"which you yet think of as singular and immaterial life!
   "Love, let it drop, let this stubborn invisible itch
"cease to torment, let it no longer drive nor distress you!
   "I Persephone send you one spray of pale blossom whose most
"fugitive odour diverts though it never would lull
   "your since transient beautiful senses which should not attempt to detain
"these bright instants which just by their fine disappearance in strife
"flex
"up and away from your fort which would bind them into your design
   "eternally dead in the would-be-vivacious vitrine."
All this she said in the second it took for her wrist
   quick to flip carelessly just as though casting a spell.
A narrative settled upon me: I gazed at the screen

with my doggedest literal stare, as though right there inside it
the thirty-two palaces of recognition should stand
    awaiting the one who should bring the decoding machine
of invincible ignorance. How they had never been kissed,
    the chimeras of plenitude: how one might stride into hell
with a harrowing glance or immediately with serene
    blessing upbraid and reveal and renew and divide it.
All who so smite shall be shown how her elegant hand
                            corrects
any who mock or forget her imperious line.
    Demeter must search for her raped and itinerant daughter and sharp
Starvation will visit hypatic republics when these
    interred and immaculate deities will to retain
those wandering spirits bound down to the cycle of slump.
    Springs shall dry up for the lack of the goddess's daughter.
Hunger shall famish the lands whence all thought have absconded:
    privation's blank temples of steel and of glass to a harp
whose impersonal musics traversing their shattered extension shall freeze
    as exorbitant junk from the orbit of money's refrain
when it clinks or it rattles disturbed in the glistering dump.
    Now it has happened and no one can find any water.
Now the sole craving which stays when the city's disbonded
                            cheques
bounce barks universally bleating and ringing the spine.
    Fats and sugars I run on are mirrored inside the light box
which sits too quite impassively here on my desk as this torrent of data
    rushes or something but not as through chasms or lava ravines
being merely the casual now unavoidable word
    chosen one day in an office for all of our mouths to palpate.
I am sitting in perfect and quite indeflectible dread.
    I am fixed in the shimmer: I quail to the tip of my socks
as the moment I always am able to put off till later
    shows me now shows me too late my judged face and my body and cleans
the velvety crimson of all lush evasions from off of the truth which is heard
    in these internal organs which will to break down but too late
to the last solidarity lullaby sung by the ignorant dead.
                            Next
enough about me but Persephone's crystalline pupils let shine
    when I met her reflected these hooves and thick antlers and she
fled down to the sources of light in the centre of earth.

Down to those unsolar fires which are parts of tellurian sun
she advanced or retreated away from me just as though meaning
    were defined as what still must elude me and what must still change
or slip slippery still more away from me more I should tighten my grip.
    Now as these worms eat my letters and natural organs I see
just how her travel is downwards decaying to birth
    or how delight in persistent refusal of fun
trills and sings sombre with ornament better than keening
    where she embellishes bases and trebles the top of her range
so that her voice plummets downwards or skipped to the tip of her lip
                              elects
the life of things which you could say is ecstatic ejection of quivering mind
    out to the lit revelation or out to the map of a world
where her song is the limit invisibly sounding design
    just at the point where mere noise is collected and hurled
triskaidekaphobic to gather us into its fine
    series of thoughts whose collective advances unfurled
still make the shape of a spirit which need not resign
    its trust to interior fortresses but whose surmises are curled
into no longer rejected dendritic adornments or nine
    banners of spirit or lights in a stone where impearled
shining of future imperilment still may refine
    word to its absolute knowing through this underworld
drowned and revived in her still disinspirited line.

                              x

Final Demand

The switch is broken. When I press
a click comes back, and nothing else.

The darkness grows around me. Tap.
Spirits assemble on the shelf.

They mock, console, revile, beseech.
They foam and founder into speech,

then they recede. It is still dark.
I look out of the window where

illuminated through a gap
glare grey expanses of the park.

The Actual Is The Rational

Grey is still grey; this calm of air
contains a part of happiness.
It is as though you were still there.
It is as though no thought of death
should ever reach me in this street,
protected by this calm, this air.

One, two, three, four, five, six and eight :
   monosyllabic seven
first integers which bring me straight
   to nine, ten, and eleven :

I count the periapts at night,
   I count them in the morning;
as though these little numbers might
   set melancholy mourning,

or mercy, pity, peace & love
   were not the human blank
but names sent kindly from above
   to open up the bank.

Erlkönig

— Mein Sohn, es ist ein Nebelstreif.

Who is that in the middle of the road?
His head is tilted slightly to one side,
not as at rest, but gripped, as if a load
pushed it for balance to the other side
from that which bears a weight. The overload
pulls down, however, from the very side
his head's skewed over to, so that both fall,
grimace and burden, to the left. A small

prederelicted strip, raised by one inch,
twelve wide, measured by me, bisects
the triple lanes of killer trucks, I flinch
at thinking how he might at one false step
greet them with body parts, a pinched
noninvitation not to walk here checks
his skipping gait which down the middle files
into the distance for three or four miles,

and he, at every step he takes, appears
about to spring with desperate delight
into their path. His rapid walk there veers
not with a trace of failing, with a light
and speedy dance, a mockery of fears
for him, and, while his mouth's screwed tight
as picturing intolerable pain
his laughing eyes redouble this again

bearing the plastic carrier towards
the blocked horizon or blank edge of this.
Gaunt, in an open shirt, he makes towards
wherever he is going. Each quick kiss
his soles click on the stone seems to award
new victories in syllogism. Hiss
from nearby tarmacs gathers to his flag.
Some burning secret is inside the bag

perhaps, or else nothing at all, just stuff
shrunk to a speck beneath the massing skies
whose clouds march darkly in grey lines of rough
hosts or slate regiments. Their void of eyes
works with vast frowns across the land. Enough
to block the very thought of light, a spies'
inverted paradise, sun, none the less,
far distant, lights them, holds them out, professed

administrators of the coming storm.
Serpents or angels seem to wriggle there
stuck with convulsion, effigies that warm
their absent excrements, meant teeth and hair,
or so, to any gaze, at least, which forms
from loss of light its lit creations where
(since, when it darkens, colours first stare out
irradiated with the shades of doubt:

no red so red as that which bleeds from cars'
retreating safety features in the gloom
when over Felixstowe the unseen stars
burn up invisibly towards their doom,
blotted, thick cloud from sight: so circles Mars,
shedding no influence at all: blank room
where this idea is entertained! you shrink
back from the lip of knowledge or lit brink

into some minor wallpapers and screens,
cooling all ardour) the darkness clasps
and rear lights sing out what their fuel means:
erased sublimity I may not grasp:
song of disowning passionately keened
where the old cosmos thinks itself the last
rotating heaven in a spirit train:
it shines: it burns & freezes: it's the same

intolerably obsolescent rock
we make grand works of artifice upon,
like this of his uncertain walk. A clock
counts up the empty minutes which have gone.
Counts up, quite needlessly, inside a locked
surveillance cabinet, the crimes foregone.
The camera sees him move from left to right.
Or does not see him, but records in light

a light-starved copy of his shining path,
passed to the one supposed to know and dumped
into the adamantine sand-bank. Harsh
cast a swept blurt of mono on the lump
of whitish, greyish screentime, a blur's bath
liming his agile pace to a spot-sump.
Only that kind of clarity was sought
which might identify him in a court.

The one supposed to know, but not to care.
The one supposed to hold in trust the worst
in order that the public's better share
should be protected from the truly cursed.
The one supposed indifferently to stare
at image after image, only at the first
which could offend, to hunt offenders down—
then to remember nothing, with a frown:

not to have looked upon the face of God,
to wipe, by rota, any poisoned trace
off from the surface of his blameless rod;
or gently wash away the once seen face
from just those lobes its image lately trod
leaving neutrality in every place:
why should I say she-he does not exist?
Why should I raise an idol, why resist

confessing the reality of Good?
Since I believe it with my skin and bones
whenever I need shelter or need food?
Since I believe it when inhuman moans
near turn to *is* evacuated *should*?
Since I believe it when the helpless stones
break from my face and stomach to the air?
Yet since I think this, why am I not there?

How can the good man man-or-woman be
an undiminished equilibrium?
How may his-her unruffled surface *see*
any disturbance in the trivium?
Composed to disenchantment: free
to entertain no true delirium?
Blind justice, gone flat blind, to sever,
right at the root, perception's nerve for ever?

These questions now depart into the air
which would accompany them with a tune
masking their proper substance. Then, just there
a raucous blare rasps out; the moon
just becomes visible; protracted care
has faltered, so one foot drops, into some gloom
some just does not take care of, till the horn
blasts a sharp reprimand into the torn

air surfaces together making up
the vast deep atmosphere around his head.
He grabs a lungful, gasps as if to sup
the doubtful vapours. It's as though these led
straight to the Real, *because* thus noxious, cupped
to his lips, bad news made good by dread:
as though the direst earth alone were just,
more strange, more terrifying, and more worth our trust.

The greys deteriorate towards their blacks.
A fine rain falls, and now that solar light
is nearly absent, the cool scarlet backs
infernally of vehicles despite
of worsened gloom declare in red the tracks
departing elsewhere, while the fronts in white
come on unvanquishably at him still
remultiplied upon a blackish rill

that mirrors to him at an instant each
accelerating core of motored cream
leaving its inauspicious tail or pleach
dressing the left air, so that each can seem
strokes of a pen upon a page they teach
not to retain the tracery they deem
perfectly fugitive. Like human life,
whatever that is, when the final knife

supposedly completes it or abolishes
its last persistences, these strings of white
sink into blackness which admonishes
a vacant face to just put out the light
in disappearance which astonishes
the optic pits along whose almost night
swim, spiral reds and iridescences,
these freed appearances from tiresome essences:

in other words, his rapt attention's put
in several places at a single time:
bound to the real appearance, hand and foot,
he stumbles, from fidelity, to chime
each curve or curlicue the light can put
back to its counterpart in reason. Rhyme
so concentrates his looking, nor diffuses
more than the pairing of his eyes refuses

the literal topography of danger.
So that, while each step topples, each corrects
the last's excess, and that, by this, each stranger,
more perilous, deviation, he thus deflects
stupid directness from its destined manger:
as, to some task, my will a stem inflects,
corroding it to new discoveries.
His walk's grand losses and recoveries

spontaneously learn their new unfreedom,
just as indefinite rehearsal brings
the lucky leaps of a delighted reason.
From the most joyful repetition springs
the purest sentiment at home in freedom:
he skips from certainty, and sheds his doubt
(a habit he has learnt to live without)

until his face is luminous with feeling
scorned and distrusted universally
whose exoteric skin components, peeling,
accompany him as he quaquaversally
may not be said to dance, yet keeling
as though in music's quick dispersal, he
trots up and strides at once with flexile arching
as though his walk were a critique of marching,

or, but less happily, the opposite
of the protracted walk he might have taken
with his dear friend, beloved opposite
whose invitation might have been mistaken
when of two paths he took the opposite
leaving his friend to feel the one forsaken:
as, on a strand but just not endless, they
might have walked down the last blue light of day

in hot pursuit of the three transcendentals,
and of their supper at the beach café,
mingling as they did then these incidentals,
some talk of Chénier, some of Dufay,
some chit-chat of the local elementals
troubling their several contentments, they
would never feel these notes or hues as bathos,
nor screw them down unduly for their pathos,

but let them parenthetically salt
all that remains implicit in a friendship
(as at that moment when the bitter talk
retrieves abraded treasures from the wrecked ship
of all lost amity, they falter, balk,
losing their footing with the aids to mend it)
as though the radiance which held to glow
at the horizon where they want to go

had been their own shared element, not love,
precisely, but involuntary hope,
having no colour but the one, above,
washed in the evening skies when gulls elope
off to wherever they are going, move
almost obliviously with each trope
or embraced counter-feint of mutual thinking:
each in each wrapped with thought's alive unshrinking

until each bears the other's argument:
all mine and yours delivered to the flood,
the learnt and the evolved integument
of lyric's logic, spluttering on mud,
as the perambulating monument
of the whole natural history of blood
letting its speculative wish and reach
run far beyond the limit of the beach

although they knew their walk was bound to end
in a cold glass, where spirits meet their ice,
yet, in idea, travel on, and send
their gazes infinitely past that nice
essential instant when the nerve will bend,
giving itself a break for once, for twice,
leaving the future's palace quite unbuilt,
and good intentions to corrode to guilt,

no, but to settle, in fidelity, to change
both less and more than one essential word:
as, from the letters which I rearrange,
or from the colours of a transposed third
a perfect repetition still finds strange
identically iterated, the blue bird
which flew past us the last time we were here.
It flies again, but wrong, since at the sheer

stroke of its quill across the evening sky
I falter, wondering whether I should say
how I'm reminded of that time, and why,
while we trudge on in silence the same way
we went the last time, plus one sacred lie,
our totem of indifference. The bay
is still there; absent, though, is I,
stuffed in the mouthpiece of our joint suppression,
and whose tongue's loosened only in digression.

Or he might not have done, who knows. His foot
works with a single twitch an elegy
of frozen elegance; his knowing boot
dismisses with one instant's energy
those possibilities, subjunctive fruit
he scorns to hunger for, a malady
he would not suffer for a single hour.
He is not sure that all those grapes are sour,

sure they are gone, and so his fleetest shoe
trips to the next stone inch of true and real
on revelation's filthy pavement. Do,
or do not mourn it, since the single reel
still rattles out from spool to spool and through
indifferently to the jet or teal
you use to decorate your cold pentameters!
Fluent or tongue-tied, orators or stammerers,

it's all one when you bite the asphalt, so
keep your eyes firmly on the headlights and
never begin to know more than you know.
Did his step say only that, or did some hand
or eyelid gesture, flung off, say, or so
I choose to seem, yet keep that happy strand
clear in my mind's eye as a silver cross?
To tell the truth some birdshit and some moss

ameliorated or depraved the grey
putting a placard up of vanquished life
or dingy recollection of the way
trod by its Afric emanation, wife,
perhaps, unsurfaced, where the hourly pay
runs out into bribed pockets, where the strife
of needs for limousines, development,
leaves it impassable. Envelopment

of wrong! He treads one harder stamp
into the earth to think of this, and bruises
his mangled left foot on an access ramp
cut out into this anti-path, then loses
security of right, and in the damp
that other limb drops, and the bent bone fuses
small shocks of rapidly communicated pain
up through his legs and body to his brain

where all such messages remain unopened
drowned or deflected by some stronger power:
since faith or narcissism blocks the open,
pushing perception down from hour to hour,
or, rather, sharpening it against each token
offered as signifying up the dour
sham re-elaboration of the facts.
Pain only ratchets for him to the max

his inability to feel it, long
since redistributed from cell to cell
inside his body's church or party, wrong
which when resummarized as good will tell
this doctrine over in a counter-song.
Cajoled by blood, like a retreating host,
they drive most violently where they the most

are self-instructed to their demolition.
Each like a superego self-inflicts
the breviary of its inanition:
each like a corporation derelicts
the chance of all alternative volition.
God on the cross! Be every globule sick!
Invent new possibilities of floundering!
May all our voyages thus float by foundering!

As a winged heart will fly from probability
so may I prosper in the happy wreck.
Or at least lose this inability
to take one hint up through my blasted neck.
The martyr-army of his self-hostility
hymned out its anthem: Just tear up the cheque!
Destroy the idol-idol-breaker, and
cut off then too your too infected hand!

Still with them march the images of bliss.
Deleted fifty times, and still more cherished
the more destroyed, a god I miss
the more I resurrect it, since I perish
infinitesimally at each kiss.
Implode or do not, everything will vanish.
The feared sky stands off in a painted black.
Expelled bad spirits offer to come back.

They sponsor quietly the public road
which curls in beauty through the countryside
(so I shall always call it) where its load
of shining tar and ash, the silver bride
jigs with delicious lightness at the code
of endless openness, as though inside
were air itself, fit to bear up this dove
whose flight's impossible as civic love

without the chthoniai. As I walked out
that morning in good spirits when the sky
shone pale blue but for pinks that round about
the dark horizon shone out into my
expectant face, still not without
their tacit rages packed down where they lie
buried imperfectly, those guarantors
murmured preserving hatreds from their floors.

Their stolen labour is my daily bread.
Their unpaid debts mount up inside my head.
Their throats inefficaciously declaim.
Their song swings back into a soundless name.
Their metals detonate the equal stamp.
Their mirrors brighter than a shining lamp.
Their broken bodies feed us, while their bones
diminish utterly beneath these stones

of whose long burials the complex map
is written out in neurones or in thoughts
quick and self-centred in the soundless gap
I live in, opening the doors and ports
to fold in multiples the knowing pap
steeped in their fluids for the is and oughts
which disappear into their secret funnel
like Kafka's dog's impenetrable tunnel:

so that his thesis, footfall's rung event,
sounds on the tarmac Alcman's choral song
gagged, bound, and cut to bits, but sent
down through the nerves of his right leg to long
for truth's own measures from the hymn they meant
(most accurately englished into Wrong)
striding thus sadly to the blissful grasses
where batteredness might find at last its arsis.

Barcarol

Awake! or get
          Up off a bed
At all events
          Sus not dead

Since I walk out
          Not unfree
More than the grass grows
          Abstractly

Or than a grey sky
          Paints its other
Streaks of day
          Same as the other

Hues of indifferent
          Colourblind
Événement
          Whose no mind

Gladdens and harbours
          One last hair
As spirit-barbers
          You prepare

Tonsured or tenured
          Then inure
To hypertrophied
          Chevelures

A boastful bouffant
          Or which skin
Worldly ascetics
          Thicken then thin

All my resuscitating
        Evohés
Dedifferentiating
           Nights from days.

Pink, vermilion
         Be the colours
Broke off a million
          Shade no duller

Than to discriminate
         One from two
Or when who
         Shatters a plate

Sees a field splinter
         Into light
So lisp a wire or
          Wrong from right

Cutting this outline
         I would know
Horse from an ox
         Or lion so

Since no cloud may
         Interpose
Or ever blur who
         Would repose

Till to a true stop
         Or real end
Means expiry
         Topped intend

Still at a gay leap
         Not abandoned
As when Semele
         Dies in tandem

Longing to burn up
        With her lover
Or just turn up
        Into clover

Whose green trefoil
        Knows no other
Song than repeating
        Luck or spoil.

At this resplendent
        Redisembarking
All dim Cythera's
        Lapdogs barking

May not howl louder
        Than the skylark
Trills dissertations
        Properly prouder

Of its demesne
        Than the sad stations
Crossed by a mark
        Both are and mean.

At this emphatic
        Non-departure
Nothing is punished
        But the martyred

Apparatus
        Sacrificially
Strangling afflatus
        Unofficially

Will on its day off
        Piss on a fire
Just for a payoff
        Eggs to mire

But as I gather
          True constraint
To an expression
          Sing or paint

Wound and blister
          To a figure
Bound and determined
          Each to sister

Rhyme or reason
          Without exception
Shedding election
          At what season

Leaves and my skin drop
          From off all faces
Tree both and body
          Spell as places.

Sleep, wake.
          Nor bless
Inauthenticable
          Happiness

More than by
          This breath
Rising and falling
          Without why

Choking no other
          When distotalled
Vacant circuits
          Broke or hover

So shining tarmacs
          Come to possession
Of all luminous
          Underexpression

Black as the best of
> False renouncers

Lit still lacking
> Western denouncers

Goggles angelic
> With inverted

Spirit-lustre
> Prereverted

To any lip
> Brushing a limit

Or null ship
> Sink and delimit.

As at a window
> Darkens a rose

Copied from neon
> Whiter than those

Petals or serifs
> Used and mentioned

Which any eye
> Blank of intention

Scatters or prints
> Over a field

Held in reversal
> Never to feel

Sugar or ink
> Descant a reason

Written in vermin
> Lost to unreason

So may optatives
> Wing from their bedded

Strip of concrete
> Implicated

Recollection
        Flight of a reach
Juster than any
        Cloudy pleach

Folded from vapour
        Into this
Waste of all colour
        Barely kissed

Or then poisoned
        By the flammable
Breath of a craft
        Writing damnable

Trails or traces
        Overhead
Whether in silver
        Or in lead.

"From a grove
        Green in dusk
Moaned a reproach
        Slow as dust.

"Top is abject.
        Spill your O.
Whether you sink,
        Swim or know

Down betters upward
        By one letter.
Rip then off this
        Left sad fetter

Till collapses
        Bleed new purple
Through all future
        Happy lapses."

But a sump who
        Was nearby
Burbled up mud's
        Brown reply.

"Blub to the gutter.
        Brace yourself.
The inner elf
        Is surplus butter.

Bray or mutter
        No more words
Than themselves splutter.
        Final surds

Make a blue
        Backlit wash.
So if you
        Wander off

No gap opens
        More than this
Panindefinite
        Inky hiss." "

Midsummer Zero

Blue shines all afternoon long and the long day's dream burns slowly
    down to its background, down to its canvas of dazzled
heat and of radiant brightnesses springing back up
    from all whites and reflectors, from metals and mirrors
and walls and the beach and the micas in wavering tarmacs,
    prone in their flat tracks pointing the cars and the cabs
through to the promenade, through to the palm-blistered strip.
    There is not not anything true here; there is not no thought
whose single attention might burn as the day burns, holding
    in flame and in fury to longing, or stuck to the nub
of some one refusal, some stubborn remainder of thought.
    Only that all the surmises can lift and float off in this weather,
lift, float and drift to wherever I want them to go,
    so that for I, I say you, or say she, when the distant
sail cuts the sealine and stitches the sea to the sky
    or it twists and then vanishes, turns, and, inviting this idle
daydream or fancy, it glistens again in the blue.

Why should I ever endure to lie down on the beach?
    Why must I fry myself here at the edge of the sea?
Some stand and undress; my face is the face of mere leisure,
    looking at nothing, the pudding of nothing, jam of it, treat
earned, the deliciously vacant extent of a workless,
    aliturgical, day, the perfection of finite privation.
It doesn't get better than this. From the strip with the palm-trees
    I look out to sea, to the wall of the numberless ocean.
I still cannot make myself see it, I cannot disperse
    except into flights and surmises and works of unfreedom.
Still in the sky I am pinned to some cloud, to some figure;
    still at the edge of the town I am staring at pictures and maps.
It is as though I believe that whatever I see
    can never have meaning, but points to a meaning elsewhere.
It is as though these white jet trails and cloud arabesques
    all in collective negation refuse their own patterns,
blanking me down to the bank of impassible blue.

Now on the strand as my gazing still falters and dips
    there pass in a gaggle the ciphers of perfect desire.
Almost as though I am already frozen or snapped
    each instant is empty of memory, love or cognition.
Almost as though I could never recall or recover
    your face and your voice, this sounding and resonant world
shrinks to a dot, to a punctual signal of wishing,
    shrinks to the total, the whole, which soon matches it, set
there like a filter or theory erasing the waters,
    set like a number which drinks them and singes them up.
Nothing can shake or discolour that number, which rages
    in superillumining purity through every part.
Hard is the colour of numbers: hard its unending identity
    counting whatever beside it is known in the world.
So as you saunter before me indifferent your nudity
    pins all attention, detains it or traps as it veils
every gesture, as though you were clothed by the sun.

Not every meaning is structured like signification.
    Not every meaning is shaped; inaudible, trackless, invisible,
it holds to itself in its pain and desire and duration.
    So when you think you have known and met truth in its nudity,
so when immediate feverish rightness would crown all your wishes,
    clothing them, burning self-evidence into the shape of a word,
sun-clear reports to the one who is clothed with the sun,
    nevertheless underneath this a mute refutation
bears and enables each false wish, as paper endures
    silently every falsehood emblazoned upon it,
silently carries the inks of unfailing negations,
    still uncomplaining awaits an intelligent lie.
If I turn round I can see the Avenses and Zephyrs
    travel or idle across or along the extended
road by the promenade, seeking their car parks and then

come to a stop where the painted line stops and the tarmac
    offers a vacancy, offers relief and a halt.
A car is too vast and expensive and brilliant even to think of.
    Even to notice it shakes every part of the blood.
So at each instant I see it I murder my wonder
    pretending that I had foreseen this, that all this is all
only some trick of the earth, that it cannot shake spirit.
    How can these colours I want to call natureless shine
except they must outshine whatever may shine in my words?
    How can I bear their perfection, their apparently deathless and nude
mass of invariant colour, their azure or bubblegum pink?
    Envy & rage bind the colours away from my sight
till I surmise them as featureless everyday stuff,
    just what is there every day when I walk down the street
holding my work of indifference in furious effort
    into my chest and my face as I try not to see what there is.
I must get on with my holiday. I must not waste any time.

Still at the last I return to the shadowless screen.
    Still I come back to the terminal screen, as if meaning
were like some reward at the end of a colourless rainbow
    or like six units of alcohol waiting for me
when I have finished composing this poem. They are some sweet
    injurious drink and appeasement to silence the talkative dead,
silence my talkative organs, my liver, my heart, and my brain.
    When these sweet numbers walk through me, I stand into panic,
hearing those voices which my being classified sane
    demands I declare to be fictions, demands that I state
always and everywhere not that I hear, but must seem to hear voices,
    seem to hear voices which urge me to works of despair.
Yes, but I hear them: yes, but they do not despair.
    I hear them demanding I help them to sound and to live.
Now the processional treads through my throat and my palate.
    Now it has come from its stations and niches and graveyards
out to this spot in the sun, where I freeze as it exits my mouth.

They depart into nothing, disperse in the limitless air.
　　Soon it will be just as though they had never been heard.
Now in the calm I can hardly hear even a word
　　staining the air, can hardly hear even a tuneful
slide or end-glide of them coming across from the sea.
　　They shall depart into numberless mountain and ocean,
they shall disperse into sky, into rivers and sea.
　　Now the remembered impossible sound of their voices
gives me the sight of your face: I shall not recover
　　compulsion of love from the feints and the trips and surmises
through to its silent and unpredeterminate name.
　　Get in the car. I can hear it: I hear its strong engine
burning the earth, and the note of its fuels and metals.
　　I no longer deafen myself with their significations,
do not for now send these tones to somebody elsewhere,
　　even as driving along by the palm-blistered strip
I try once again not to use the wrong side of the road.

Acknowledgements

Some of these poems have previously appeared in the following publications: *Chicago Review*, *half-circle*, *nonsite*, *PN Review*, *plantarchy.us*, *Programme of the Second Sussex Poetry Festival*, *the claudius app*. My thanks to their editors.